I am a big cat!

By Camilla de la Bedoyere

Miles Kelly

Look out for the 'Ask for help!' boxes. You will need help from an adult to do these activities.

Ask for help!

Answers from pages 16–17

Jumble in the jungle
1. Leopard
2. Lion
3. Tiger
4. Cheetah

Clever cat
1. A pride
2. Spots
3. The cheetah

Whose cub?
Christina

Spot count
The most spots: Laurence
The least spots: Leah

Odd one out
a. Tusk
b. Feather
c. Fly

First published in 2014 by Miles Kelly Publishing Ltd
Harding's Barn, Bardfield End Green, Thaxted, Essex, CM6 3PX, UK
Copyright © Miles Kelly Publishing Ltd 2014

10 9 8 7 6 5 4 3 2 1

Publishing Director Belinda Gallagher
Creative Director Jo Cowan
Editorial Director Rosie Neave
Assistant Editor Amy Johnson
Designers Jo Cowan, Venita Kidwai
Image Manager Liberty Newton
Production Manager Elizabeth Collins
Reprographics Stephan Davis, Jennifer Cozens, Thom Allaway, Lorraine King, Anthony Cambray

ISBN 978-1-78209-505-7

Printed in China

British Library Cataloguing-in-Publication Data
A catalogue record for this book is available from the British Library

ACKNOWLEDGEMENTS

The publishers would like to thank Joe Jones and Richard Watson (Bright Agency) for the illustrations they contributed to this book.
All other artwork from the Miles Kelly Artwork Bank.

The publishers would like to thank the following sources for the use of their photographs:
t = top, b = bottom, l = left, r = right, c = centre,
bg = background, rt = repeated throughout

Cover (front) Sergey Gorshkov/Minden Pictures/FLPA; (back, cl, tr) Eric Isselee/Shutterstock
Corbis 21(b) Andrew Parkinson
Dreamstime 5(cr) Musat; 11(t) Seread
FLPA 10 Jurgen & Christine Sohns; 13(tr) Ariadne Van Zandbergen
Fotolia 9(panel, t) Irochka
iStock 5(tr) MarieHolding; 12 ACS15
Nature Picture Library 4–5 Edwin Giesbers; 13(tl) Anup Shah; 15(t) Sandesh Kadur; 18–19 Andy Rouse
Shutterstock Heading panel (rt) Chris Kruger; Joke panel (rt) Tropinina Olga; Learn a Word panel (rt) donatas1205; Learn a Word cartoon (rt) Virinaflora; 1 Eric Isselee; 2 Envita; 3(r) Eric Isselee; 5(br) FloridaStock; 6 Stu Porter; 7(t) Dennis Donohue, (b) Sean Nel; 8–9(bg) Petrov Stanislav; 8(panel, tl) Ambient Ideas, (br) tachyglossus, (panel, tr) Anna Tsekhmister, (tr); 9(heading panel, tl) sharpner, (heading, b) Lyolya; 11(r) Boleslaw Kubica; 13(bl) Andreas Doppelmayr; 14(l and r) Eric Isselee; 15(b) Krzysztof Wiktor; 16–17(bg) Lucy Baldwin; 16(c) andere andrea petrlik, (panel, b) donatas1205; 17(bl) Memo Angeles, (panels, br) LittleRambo; 19(b) Matt Hart; 20 Chris Kruger; 21(t) Magnus Haese
Stickers (cheetah, tr) John T Takai/Shutterstock, (jumping cat, cr) andere andrea petrlik/Shutterstock

Every effort has been made to acknowledge the source and copyright holder of each picture. Miles Kelly Publishing apologizes for any unintentional errors or omissions.

Made with paper from a sustainable forest

www.mileskelly.net
info@mileskelly.net

Contents

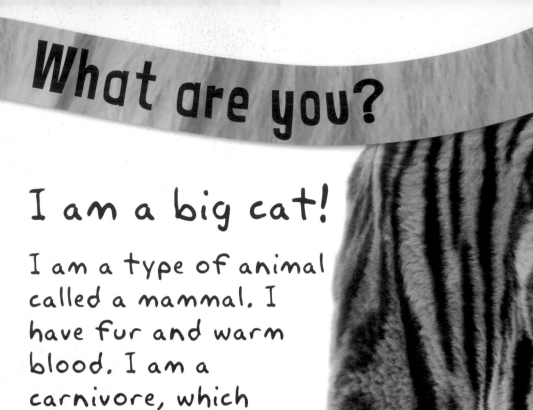

I am a big cat!

I am a type of animal called a mammal. I have fur and warm blood. I am a carnivore, which means I eat other animals.

Long tail

Siberian tiger

Q. What is a lion's favourite meal?

A. Baked beings on toast!

Lions, tigers, leopards and cheetahs are all big cats.

Thick, soft fur

Whiskers

Paws with sharp claws

Small cats

Some wild cats are much smaller than big cats. Their size means they are fast and good at climbing.

Caracal

Ocelot

Lynx

How do you hunt?

I chase other animals!

I use my big jaws and
sharp claws to grab them.
All big cats have
strong senses.
We can see, hear
and smell other
animals from
far away.

Q. What did the lion
say to the gazelle?

A. Pleased to eat you!

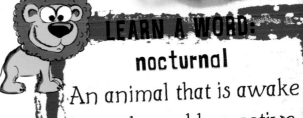

Pouncing

Giant leap

Pumas have very strong back legs and can leap a long way. They sometimes pounce on their prey from above.

LEARN A WORD:
nocturnal
An animal that is awake at night and less active during the day.

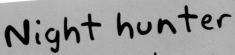

Creeping

Night hunter

Most big cats are nocturnal. Lions, tigers and leopards hunt at night. In the dark, they can creep up on other animals.

Activity time

Get ready to make and do!

Draw me!

YOU WILL NEED: pencils · paper

1. Draw a wide oval for the body and a circle for the head.

2. Add two lines for the neck. Draw the legs and tail.

3. Draw two rounded ears. Add the nose, mouth and eyes.

Quiet as a cat

One person is Big Cat and faces a wall. The players must creep towards Big Cat. When Big Cat hears someone move he roars, and the players start again. To win, a player must reach Big Cat without being heard.

Now colour me in and give me a name!

Big cat card

YOU WILL NEED:
A4 card · scissors · glitter
coloured pens and pencils

HERE'S HOW:
1. Fold the card in half and draw the outline of a tiger on one side. Make sure that both the head and tail reach the fold.
2. Cut out the tiger, leaving the folds at the head and tail.

3. Decorate your card.

YOU WILL NEED:
cupcakes · popcorn · knife
orange or yellow icing
black icing in a piping bag

HERE'S HOW:
1. Cover the top of each cake with orange or yellow icing and smooth it with the side of the knife.

2. Put popcorn around the edge of the cake to make a mane.
3. Use the black icing to draw the eyes, the nose, the mouth and the whiskers.

9

Where do you live?

Sumatran tiger

I live in the hot jungle.

When it gets too hot I take a cooling dip in the river. There is lots of shade from the trees where I can rest.

Cold and snow

Snow leopards have thick fur to keep them warm in their mountain home. They hunt sheep and hares.

Q. What is striped and bouncy?

A. A tiger on a trampoline!

Tree cat

Leopards are good at climbing trees. They often hide their food in the branches. These big cats live in grasslands, forests, mountains and deserts.

African leopard

What are your babies called?

My babies are called cubs!

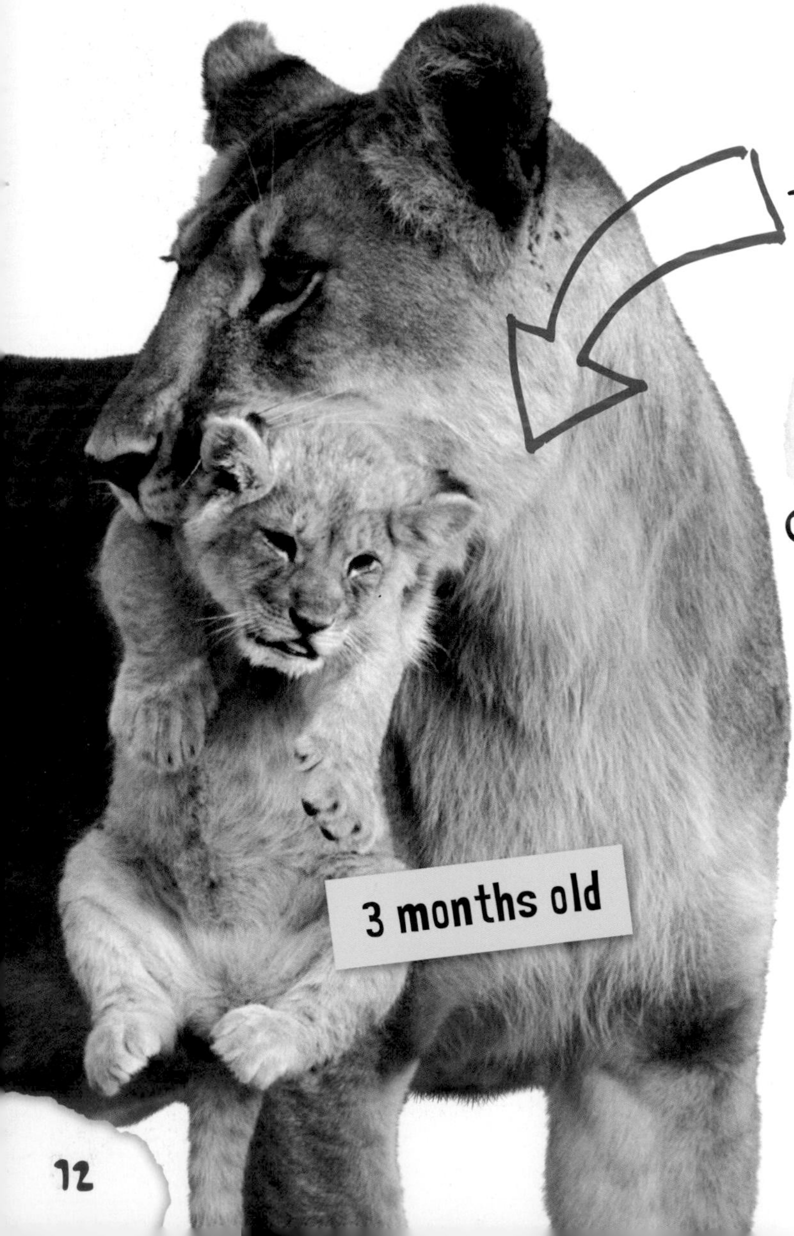

1

Cubs are born blind and helpless. Their mother feeds them with milk.

Newborn

3 months old

2

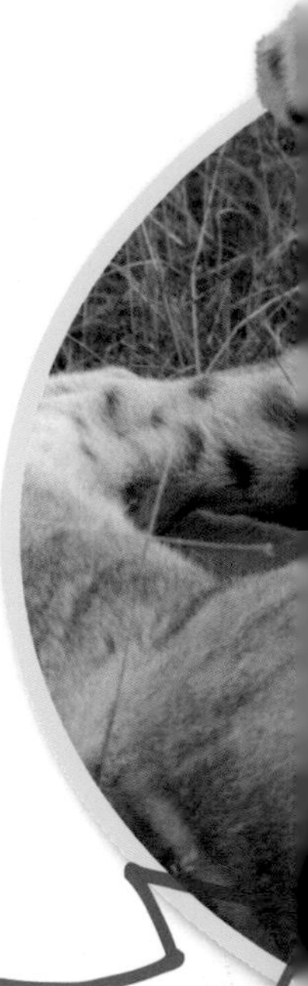

Cubs rely on their mother for food and safety. She can move them quickly if they are in danger, by carrying them in her mouth.

Family life

Lions live in family groups called prides. Every lion in the pride helps to look after the cubs.

One year old

3
Cubs love to play-fight. It helps them learn to hunt, and makes them stronger as they grow up.

Q. What happened to the leopard who spent too long in the bath?
A. He was spotless!

What do you look like?

Black panther

Leopard

I am spotty.

All leopards have spots.
Leopards or jaguars that
have dark fur are known
as black panthers. Their
spots can still be seen.

Q. What did the tiger say when he looked in the mirror?

A. Purr-fect!

Hard to spot

Tigers have stripy coats. This helps them to hide in long, dry grass and in the shadowy jungle.

Clouded wonder

This cat has cloud-shaped markings on its fur. Clouded leopards are shy cats, and very rare.

Puzzle time

Can you solve all the puzzles?

Clever cat

1. What is a lion family called – a pride or a pack?
2. Do leopards have spots or stripes?
3. Which cat runs fastest – the puma or the cheetah?

Jumble in the jungle

Can you unscramble these big cat names?

1. PARLEOD
2. ILON
3. GIRET
4. HEETCHA

Whose cub?

Which cheetah parent has left Charlie the cub behind? Trace the path back to find out.

Chelsea

Chester

Christina

Charlie

Spot count

Count each leopard's spots. Who has the most, and who has the least?

Laurence

Lisa

Leah

Odd one out

Can you find the odd one out in each box?

fang
tooth
tusk
jaws

a

stripe
fur
whisker
feather

b

fly   run
climb   jump

c

Find the answers on page 2.

How fast can you run?

Cheetah

I am super speedy!

I can sprint faster than any other animal in the world, but only for short distances. My speed helps me when I am hunting.

Q. Which cat always wins at card games?
A. The cheetah!

LEARN A WORD:

swamp

A place with wet, boggy ground.

Super swimmer

Jaguars live near swamps and rivers. They are strong swimmers. They hunt animals such as turtles and alligators in water.

19

I roar to scare other animals.

My roar is so loud that other animals can hear me from far away. It warns them to keep out of my space.

Q. What happened when the lion ate the clown?

A. He felt funny!

Jaws and claws

Cheetahs have big jaws, long fangs and sharp claws! Their claws help them to grip the ground as they run.

Cat fights

Big cats fight over food, mates and space. They do not like to share!

21

The Lion that Couldn't Roar

Use your stickers to illustrate the story

The day that Stanley was born was a proud day for his family. He was a strong cub, with sharp claws and big teeth.

His mother and father said that he would be the leader of a pride, stronger than all other lions.

"Meow!" answered Stanley.

His mother and father looked at each other in horror. "Stanley can't roar!" they cried.

The next day, Stanley went to see Wise Buffalo in the forest. "Will I ever be able to roar?" he asked.

The Wise Buffalo looked thoughtful. At last he said, "You will never roar, unless you have faith in yourself."

"I have never heard of faith-in-yourself," said Stanley. "But I shall find it." He returned to the grassland and asked everyone where to look.

"Search underground," suggested Aardvark, poking his head out from his cool, dark burrow.

"Look in a book," said Baboon, who read lots.

"It will be somewhere far away," said who gazed over the treetops.

So Stanley dug a hole in the dirt. He read Baboon's books and he climbed to the top of a tree and looked far away. Still, he could not roar.

That night, Stanley was so tired from looking

for faith-in-yourself that he didn't notice he was sleeping with his head on a termite mound. As he slept, the furious termites emerged from their nest. The termite queen told all the bugs to climb over Stanley. Then she counted, "Three – two – one, go!", and all the termites bit Stanley as hard as they could with their little jaws.

"ROOOAAAAAAR!" Stanley let out the loudest roar that had ever been heard on the grassland. It even woke up Wise Buffalo. "Sounds like Stanley had faith in himself after all!" he said.

By Camilla de la Bedoyere